Plants

Plant ABC

Patricia Whitehouse

Heinemann Library
Chicago, Illinois

Designed by Sue Emerson/Heinemann Library, Page layout by Carolee A. Biddle
Printed and bound in the U.S.A. by Lake Book

06 05 04 03 02
10 9 8 7 6 5 4 3 2 1

Library of Congress Cataloging-in-Publication Data
Whitehouse, Patricia, 1958-
  Plant ABC / Patricia Whitehouse.
    p. cm. — (Plants)
Includes index.
Summary: Illustrates "a" for apple, "j" for jasmine, and "z" for zucchini, along with brief explanatory text about various plants.
  ISBN 1-58810-522-9 (HC), 1-58810-733-7 (Pbk.)
  1. Plants—Juvenile literature. [1. Plants. 2. Alphabet.] I. Title.
II. Plants (Des Plaines, Ill.)
  QK49 .W53 2002
  580—dc21

2001003654

Acknowledgments
The author and publishers are grateful to the following for permission to reproduce copyright material:
p. 3L E. R. Degginger; p. 3R Rick Wetherbee; pp. 4, 10, 16, 17, 23b, 23c, 23k Dwight Kuhn; p. 5 Craig Mitchelldyer; pp. 6, 23a Tom Edwards/Visuals Unlimited; p. 7 Mark E. Gibson/Visuals Unlimited; pp. 8L, 8R Dick James; pp. 9, 23j Eda Rogers; p. 11 Amor Montes De Oca; pp. 12L, 21 Winston Fraser; pp. 12R, 23e Jerome Wexler/Visuals Unlimited; p. 13 Science Vu/Visuals Unlimited; p. 14 Carol and Don Spencer/Visuals Unlimited; pp. 15, 23h Greg Ryan/Sally Beyer; p. 18 Jeffrey Rich Nature Photography; p. 19 Marv Binegar; pp. 20, 23f Inga Spence/Visuals Unlimited; pp. 22L, 23i James M. Mejuto; p. 22R, 23l Phil Degginger/Color Pic, Inc.; pp. 23d, 23g Dick James

Cover photographs courtesy of (L–R): Dwight Kuhn; Inga Spence/Visuals Unlimited; Dwight Kuhn

Every effort has been made to contact copyright holders of any material reproduced in this book. Any omissions will be rectified in subsequent printings if notice is given to the publisher.

Special thanks to our advisory panel for their help in the preparation of this book:
Eileen Day, Preschool Teacher
Chicago, IL

Paula Fischer, K–1 Teacher
Indianapolis, IN

Sandra Gilbert,
Library Media Specialist
Houston, TX

Angela Leeper,
Educational Consultant
North Carolina Department
of Public Instruction
Raleigh, NC

Pam McDonald, Reading Teacher
Winter Springs, FL

Melinda Murphy,
Library Media Specialist
Houston, TX

Helen Rosenberg, MLS
Chicago, IL

Anna Marie Varakin,
Reading Instructor
Western Maryland College

The publishers would also like to thank Anita Portugal, a master gardener at the Chicago Botanic Garden, for her help in reviewing the contents of this book for accuracy.

Some words are shown in bold, **like this.**
You can find them in the picture glossary on page 23.

A a   Apple
B b   Blackberry

Apples have seeds inside.

Blackberries have seeds inside, too.

C c   Carrot

The orange part of a carrot
is its **root**.

D d   Dirt
E e   Eat

Some roots grow in the dirt.

People and animals eat roots.

F f　Fruit

Seeds grow inside the **fruit**.

G g Garden

A garden is a place to grow flowers.

H h   Hyacinth
I i   Iris

hyacinth

iris

Some people grow **hyacinths** and **irises** in their gardens.

Jj   Jasmine

Jasmine flowers smell sweet.

K k   Kale

Kale is a leafy plant that people eat.

Ll   Lettuce

People eat the leaves of lettuce
plants, too.

M m   Mango
N n   Nectarine

nectarine

seed

mango

Mangoes and nectarines have only one seed inside.

O o   Orange

seed

Oranges have many seeds inside.

P p Palm

A palm tree is a kind of plant.

Q q Quaking Aspen

A **quaking aspen** is a kind of tree.

Its leaves shake even in a small breeze.

R r   Root

Roots grow under the ground.

S s   Stem

stem

Stems grow above the ground.

Tt   Tree Trunk

This tree trunk is very big.

U u   Up

You have to look up to see the
top of this tree.

V v   Vein

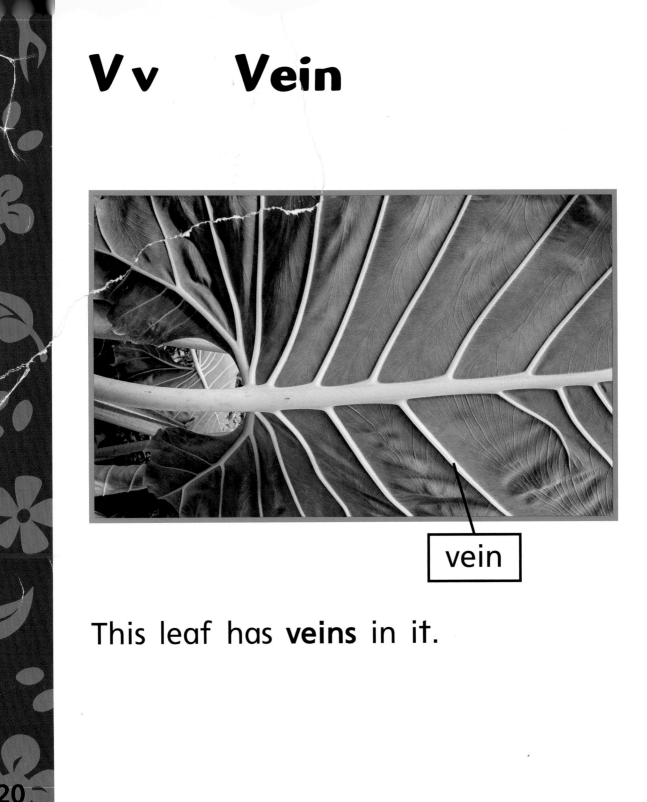

vein

This leaf has **veins** in it.

Ww Water
Xx Examine

Water moves through the veins of a leaf.

Examine the leaf's veins with a magnifying glass.

Y y Yucca
Z z Zucchini

yucca

zucchini

Some **yucca** plants grow where it is dry.

Zucchini plants grow where there is a lot of rain.

Picture Glossary

fruit
page 6

kale
page 10

stem
page 17

hyacinth
(HI-a-sinth)
page 8

mango
page 12

vein
pages 20, 21

iris
(EYE-ris)
page 8

quaking aspen
(KWAY-king AS-pen)
page 15

yucca
(YUCK-a)
page 22

jasmine
(JAZ-min)
page 9

root
pages 4, 5, 16

zucchini
(zoo-KEE-nee)
page 22

Note to Parents and Teachers

Using this book, children can practice alphabetic skills while learning interesting facts about plants. Together, read *Plant ABC.* Say the names of the letters aloud, then say the target word, exaggerating the beginning of the word. For example, "/r/: Rrrrrr-oot." Can the child think of any other words that begin with the /r/ sound? (Although the letter x is not at the beginning of the word "examine," the /ks/ sound of the letter x is still prominent.) Try to sing the "ABC Song," substituting the plant alphabet words for the letters a, b, c, and so on.

Index